KIBBLE

The Palace

ROBERT COWIE

AuthorHouse™ UK
1663 Liberty Drive
Bloomington, IN 47403 USA
www.authorhouse.co.uk
UK TFN: 0800 0148641 (Toll Free inside the UK)
UK Local: 02036 956322 (+44 20 3695 6322 from outside the UK)

This book is printed on acid-free paper.

ISBN: 978-1-7283-7976-0 (sc)
ISBN: 978-1-7283-7975-3 (e)

Print information available on the last page.

Published by AuthorHouse 12/28/2022

authorHOUSE®

Dedication

To Michelle Carty for sifting through a mind-numbing selection of photos to help me find fifty.

To Rachel Mills my incredibly patient art tutor for doing the front cover artwork.

And in loving memory of my partner, Jacqueline Schindler, recently passed, who would love to have seen me actually finishing something. I trust she is in a much more iridescent and happy crystal palace.

KIBBLE
The Palace

This is a totally subjective book of photographs of a treasured Glasgow icon within another amazing place known to all Glaswegians, the Botanical Gardens. The gardens and the palace seem to perfectly merge into each other in a totally seamless pattern of perfect harmony.

When I say subjective, I mean it's my impressions in photos. It's something of what I feel for the place, as it's been a part of much of my life.

I could have gone down the road of doing a somewhat technical manual and history, but that is well covered anyway. Tempted to do an explanation of each shot, I decided it was more fun for the reader/viewer to form their own impressions and thoughts.

Keeping it subjective, I would love to have been around when it was floated up on a barge from Coulport near Helensburgh and up to Glasgow from John Kibble's place. I marvel that they didn't break it. Although it was recently dismantled, renovated and strengthened and looks even grander and in better nick than before.

Kibble was an eccentric polymath whom I'd love to have met—well he did try to cycle across a local loch on a bike with floats—and I am so glad his grand ideas gave rise to the core part of this structure. I must give his architects and engineers a huge vote of thanks for creating what I consider to be a miraculous building. I have spent my working life

with architects and engineers, so forgive me, I have not taken this path here.

From a tot of about four years, the Botanics, as we all call them here, was really my garden. My family lived locally, and we had a postage stamp type of back garden. Victorians didn't sit around sunbathing, but I think preferred to promenade in parks. My brother and I constantly clamoured to go to the Botanics.

We weren't much interested in plants, although the huge interior of giant Australasian ferns and palm-like trees were like a magical jungle to little boys, both spooky and mysterious! Our cry was usually, 'Can we go and see the goldfish!' If someone had called them carp we would have been flummoxed. How can a carp be a goldfish? It has no romance.

I still wander around this magical, mystical place in awe and amazement. It quietens me. It's like a glass cathedral, a place of peace and serenity, and there is something eternal about it.

I visited the world's oldest rainforest in Australia, and the lush foliage in the Kibble takes me back there. The difference being there is nothing in the Kibble to kill or maim you. And you can't disappear forever, although there is something of another dimension in the Kibble.

To myself, the fashion in which it is laid out is perfect too, a harmonious blend of a floating glass light with the structure appearing lightweight and wonderful. Sculptures that intrigue all complimented by magnificent flowers and lush greenery.

For some fun I will list the various sculptures, and you can name them for yourselves. For the flora, get your phone plant apps out and have more fun.
The statues are:
King Robert of Sicily by Paulin
Cain by Mellins
Eve by Tadolini
Ruth by Ciniselli
The Sisters of Bethany by Wood
The Elf by Gascombe John.
I have attended many functions here, musical, theatre and art, plus others. The acoustics aren't perfect, but the setting far outweighs that. Imagine having a wedding here!

I have been to grand buildings and palaces all over the world, and whilst many have been magnificent, this will always be my palace. I'll conclude with heartfelt thanks to Artist Rachel Mills, for her brilliant input, and for giving this scribbler art tutoring, and not losing her cool.

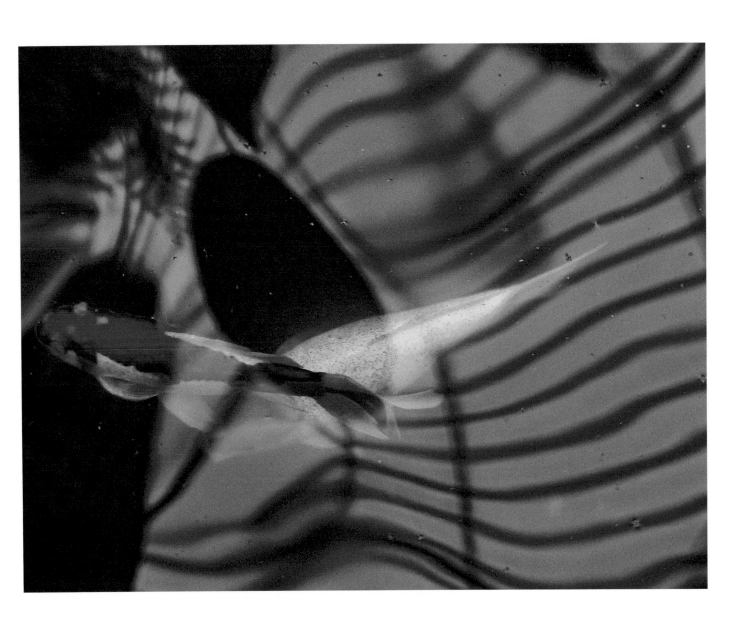

Robert Cowie

Robert Cowie

Printed in the United States
by Baker & Taylor Publisher Services